The Old Wolf
and
The Little Red Hen

For Reading Practice with *Ellie's Code*

Level 2

by **ELIANA VILLARROEL**

Illustrated by

Mauricio Sanchez-Patzy

Ellie's Code

Text and illustrations copyright © 2008 by Eliana Villarroel

ISBN 978-0-9911507-3-1

Summary and Directions:

The research-based method used in Ellie's Code is designed to teach children and older non-readers, including those with reading and spelling difficulties, learning disabilities, and English language learners, to decode, build fluency, and develop spelling accuracy.

Color-coded words aid and guide the brain to recognize mini-words within words and spelling patterns to process faster. This develops automaticity leading to greater fluency.

The readers will be delighted to follow the wolf on his adventure to find the Little Red Hen. The wolf's quest and determination to be accepted and his attempts to make new friends is endearing and humorously entertaining. At first, Little Red Hen does not trust Old Wolf and bravely tries to protect her chicks and herself. Soon after that, she realizes that this wolf is different! Old Wolf manages to gain Little Red Hen's trust by offering his services to help around the farm doing chores. The reader will be pleasantly surprised to find out how two incompatible characters manage to become great friends.

Using this color-coded method allows the reader to discover a unique, simple method to decode and spell the English language with ease and enjoyment.

This Level 2 story is recommended for second through third grade level students. **Old Wolf and Jack and the Beanstalk** is a Level 3 color-coded sequel story for third through fifth grade level readers. **Old Wolf's Search for Pinocchio** is a Level 4 color-coded sequel story designed to improve reading fluency for sixth grade level readers and beyond.

For eight years, this method was thoroughly tested and successfully used with hundreds of special education students, English language learners, and students who were identified at risk because of their inability to read and write at grade level.

After approximately 30 hours of instruction, the average reading fluency growth had an increase of 39 words per minute. Grade level reading fluency tests with black text were used to determine progress. All participants came from first through fifth grade levels. Students who participated in the program were first identified as being far below basic or below basic in reading fluency. Students made an easy transition from the color-coded material to all black text.

Ellie's Code

SUMMARY GUIDE FOR COLOR-CODE USAGE:

COLOR CODE:	USE:	SAMPLES:
BLUE LETTER (S)	■ Identify whole words or mini-words within word(s) and/or spelling patterns which can be easily decoded in isolation.	as, fast, has, all, call, can, the, them, for, only, just, think, story, together, watch, you, before
GREEN LETTER (S)	■ Complete all the sounds required to decode the word when added to the blue letters and/or the blue and red letters.	they, was, about, maybe, words, ants
	■ May serve to identify the change of nouns from singular to plural.	legs, pigs, bricks
	■ Regular verb-tense endings: (present progressive, past tense)	doing, falling, saying, looked, called
	■ Adverb endings as needed.	luckily, proudly
RED LETTER (S)	■ Identify silent letter(s). Important to remember for spelling.	one, why, know, watch, school, answered
	■ May alert the reader to change the previous vowel(s) sound from a short vowel to a long vowel, or vice versa.	time, made, like, give, have
	■ Guides the reader to focus on decoding the blue short/long vowel while ignoring the red vowel for vowel digraphs (two successive letters whose phonetic value is a single sound).	your, yours, could, please, people, thought, because
	■ Help to distinguish the correct meaning of a homophone (Two or more words pronounced alike but are different in meaning, derivation or spelling.)	to, too, two right, write their, there hear, here

This story is dedicated to the loving memory of my great-aunt

MARIA PEGOTTINI,

a gifted story teller and a superb woman.

Her original stories created a fascinating and entertaining world of

imaginative characters that cradled and nurtured

my childhood memories.

This story began nine days after the poor old wolf's tail had finally healed from a terrible accident. The day of the accident had been dreadful for the wolf. He had fallen into a pot of hot water at the Three Little Pigs' house.

The wolf was still lonely and wanted to find a friend he could trust. He had not stopped thinking about visiting the Little Red Hen. "She strikes me as a nice hen: hard working, clean, owns her house, and a great cook, on top of all that! I must not forget that she also lays eggs! That will come in handy to supply my need for protein in my new vegetarian diet." The wolf drew upon his strength and courage to venture out again into the woods, across the hills, and beyond the meadows straight to the Little Red Hen's house.

The sun was rising, the birds were singing, and there was not a single cloud in the sky. The old wolf put on his clean pants. Then he looked in the mirror and straightened out his whiskers. He smiled and said to himself, "I may be old, but I am still

strong, charming, polite, and a great companion for anyone smart enough to appreciate all I offer!"

He took a deep breath, gathered some fresh corn, and with a cheerful attitude and a bright smile, he quickly went out of his den to find a new friend. Huffing and puffing, puffing and huffing, he walked through the woods, up the hills, and down to the meadow. This was not an easy walk nor was the path short, but for this old wolf, it was a wonderful trek.

After a while, the wolf stopped on the meadow to gather a bunch of flowers. He rolled on the grass and amused himself chasing butterflies and dragonflies. All of a sudden, he started sneezing and wheezing. The spring pollen in the air either was bringing back his allergies or causing him to have an asthma attack.

The sneezing and wheezing wolf ran to the stream to soak his nose in the running water. Not long after that, he was knocking on Little Red Hen's front door.

At first, no one answered, so he put his ear close to the door, but all he could hear was the dog snoring. The old wolf looked through the window and saw the cat cuddled up, taking a nap. When he turned around, he almost stepped on the yellow duck. The old wolf inquired as to the whereabouts of the Little Red Hen, but to his disbelief, all this yellow fellow could say was, "Quack, quack!"

The wolf decided to follow the yellow fellow to the backyard where the Little Red Hen was working hard tilling the land. She looked surprised and a bit apprehensive when she saw the yellow duck leading the wolf straight to her garden.

The Little Red Hen grabbed her hoe and thought to herself, "Only a dumb duck would do such a thing as to bring an old wolf to my garden! I hope the wolf is not hungry nor does he try to trick me." Then she courageously shouted, loudly commanding, "Stop in your tracks, you tricky old wolf! I may be just a chicken, but I am not about to become your *polla loca*! I will

put up a brave fight all the way to the end to save my baby chicks and protect my neck!"

The old wolf grinned nervously, apologizing for the intrusion and the abrupt surprise. He said politely, "Please put down your weapon, Little Red Hen. I mean no harm to you or your chicks. I came a long way just for a friendly visit. I heard your wheat is not ready for harvesting, and out of concern, I wanted to share a good meal of corn which I have carefully selected. If you care to trust me, I have it right here in my basket."

The Little Red Hen looked relieved, but was not totally convinced of the wolf's good intentions. She needed some proof as to the purpose of his visit before she could trust him. "Why should I trust you, old wolf? You have a bad reputation and I don't know what your true intentions are," said the Little Red Hen.

The old wolf tried to be poised, pretended to be cool, and gallantly handed the pretty bouquet of flowers

4

he had gathered for the Little Red Hen. As he handed the flowers to her, he started to sneeze. His allergies were back and he started to wheeze. Crying, wheezing, and sneezing, the poor old wolf broke down. He began to explain how lonely he felt and how he just wanted to have a good friend. The Little Red Hen's heart started to melt. The flowers and tears had done the trick. She put down the hoe, took off her apron, and helped the poor old wolf to wipe his tears and blow his nose.

Before long, they were both at the house drinking a cup of chamomile tea and eating corn on the cob. Just like old friends, they shared stories of days gone by. The old wolf told her about his unpleasant ordeal at the Three Little Pigs' house. He even showed her the scar on his tail to prove the truth of his accident and to be more convincing about that horrible, terrible, most frightful day!

QUACK!!
QUACK!!

The Little Red Hen complained about the lazy dog she had picked up by the side of the road. She told the old wolf how the dog had promised to earn his keep by chasing the crows and protecting the house. But once he became accustomed to a free meal, all he provided was an occasional bark and an insatiable appetite. "Now I don't have the heart to throw this old dog back to the road. He is not much bother and he is a nice dog, but he never wants to do any work!" lamented the Little Red Hen.

Then she mentioned the sleepy cat who had promised to chase away the rats and the mice, but once the cat became accustomed to a free meal, he slept all day long. However, he was polite and always remembered to purr, showing gratitude for his daily cup of milk and can of sardines. "I cannot ask him to leave. Who knows what could happen to him alone in this world? This poor cat says he is nocturnal by nature and can only work at night. He claims that he desperately needs to rest during the day or that he will fall apart.

However, he cannot work at night, either, because it is too cold or damp, which would only aggravate his arthritis and rheumatism! In spite of all that, he is such a wonderful and loving cat!" the Little Red Hen sighed.

Finally, she pointed to the noisy yellow duck and explained how this poor fellow had been labeled the "Ugly Duckling" and was chased out of his pond by a group of conceited and arrogant swans. She obviously had a good heart because she had kept him around the house in spite of his constant and annoying, "Quack, quack!"

She proceeded to explain how someone had made the yellow duck believe that someday he would turn into a beautiful white swan. Then she added, "This poor duck needs to understand and accept the fact that he is just a plain old duck! This business about turning into something you are not is nothing but a fairy tale wish or a plastic surgeon's propaganda. I do not understand why, after a year, his feathers are still yellow. I think this poor fellow just doesn't want to grow up. I would

be happier if he could at least talk and learn to be helpful around the house instead of quacking all day! There are too many chores to do in the garden and in the house! No one wants to help me!"

The clever old wolf got the hint. He did not waste this opportunity and started to explain how he had all the necessary skills and qualifications to help the distraught Little Red Hen. "Take a good look at my pointy claws, Little Red Hen! I can dig up the ground for you in the wink of an eye! Take a good look at my long snout, pretty henny! I can drag the old hose to water your garden at the snap of your toes! Take a good look at my sharp teeth, sweetie pie! I can cut the wheat faster than you can wiggle your beak! Take a good look at my strong muscles, honey bunch! I can carry the wheat to the mill and be back before any rooster can crow at dawn! All I ask in return is for a place to sleep, and instead of bread, if you could please make pizza every day!"

The Little Red Hen was cautiously impressed and decided to give the poor old wolf a chance to prove himself. The months passed by and all went well. Every day he ate boiled eggs for breakfast and pizza for lunch and dinner! That food gave the poor old wolf indigestion with hiccups and heartburn. He could not sleep anymore!

But after a year, the old wolf grew tired of the routine and found himself growing restless again. Sleep deprivation started to make his mind wonder what might lay yonder beyond the hills and far away mountains. He stared at the full moon and felt the call of the wild. He had to make a decision whether or not to follow his intuition.

Little Red Hen understood when the day came and her good friend had to go away. She watched sadly as he folded and packed his clothes. The wolf tried in vain to explain how he had heard the news about a foolish boy named Jack who had traded his last cow for a handful of beans! The old wolf needed a new

adventure and this was the perfect excuse to leave by saying, "It is a wolf's duty to come to the rescue of a foolish boy and his poor mother. I must use my expertise to show them how to plant and grow great beans. Duty calls me and I must go immediately to a far away land. No time must be wasted; I must leave in haste!"

They said their good-byes. The Little Red Hen cried. Her chicks were upset because they were fond of the wolf. They would miss playing hide-and-go-seek and being cradled to sleep listening to his wolf time stories. The lazy dog howled sadly and the sleepy cat sobbed inconsolably. The noisy yellow duck was depressed and showed his grief with just one soft quiet "Quack." Even the old wolf had tears in his eyes and a runny nose. He had just started to feel remorse for leaving his good friends. This made him want to cry, but he tried to pretend that his allergies were coming back.

Before he could change his mind, the wolf quickly thanked the Little Red Hen for giving him a chance and being a great hostess throughout the long year. But most of all, thanked her for being his best friend. The wolf hugged each of the animals, promising to come back someday, and then he turned to disappear in the wink of an eye. Over the meadows and beyond the skyline, the clever old fellow was on his way to a far away land.

www.ingramcontent.com/pod-product-compliance
Lightning Source LLC
Chambersburg PA
CBHW060816090426
42737CB00002B/86